FISHKEEPER'S GUIDE TO
WATER GARDENING

By Derek Lambert

My own interest in coldwater fish keeping started way back when I was only a small child and won a Goldfish at the local fair. At the time it was a common sight to see Goldfish offered as prizes for games of chance or skill, and they could normally be seen hanging in small polythene bags from the ceiling of the booth. Even though I was a small child at the time, I thought keeping Goldfish in such cramped conditions was cruel and set out to rescue as many as possible. I lost more often than I won, but we still ended up with quite a number of Goldfish and nowhere to put them.

My parents were wonderful about this sort of thing and kindly bought an aquarium for the "rescuees". Looking back on it now, it was far too small for the number of fish in it, but it tided them over until a pond made its appearance.

This was installed one Saturday afternoon and by the evening the fish were transferred into it, together with two new ones my brother and I had bought earlier in the day, by the evening. Raw tapwater, without a water conditioner, was used to fill our new pond, but remarkably the fish survived it and remained healthy.

Distributed in the UNITED STATES to the Pet Trade by T.F.H. Publications, Inc., One T.F.H. Plaza, Neptune City, NJ 07753; on the Internet at www.tfh.com; in CANADA Rolf C. Hagen Inc., 3225 Sartelon St. Laurent-Montreal Quebec H4R 1E8; Pet Trade by H & L Pet Supplies Inc., 27 Kingston Crescent, Kitchener, Ontario N2B 2T6; in ENGLAND by T.F.H. Publications, PO Box 15, Waterlooville PO7 6BQ; in AUSTRALIA AND THE SOUTH PACIFIC by T.F.H. (Australia), Pty. Ltd., Box 149, Brookvale 2100 N.S.W., Australia; in NEW ZEALAND by Brooklands Aquarium Ltd. 5 McGiven Drive, New Plymouth, RD1 New Zealand; in SOUTH AFRICA, Rolf C. Hagen S.A. (PTY.) LTD. P.O. Box 201199, Durban North 4016, South Africa; in Japan by T.F.H. Publications, Japan—Jiro Tsuda, 10-12-3 Ohjidai, Sakura, Chiba 285, Japan. Published by T.F.H. Publications, Inc.

MANUFACTURED IN THE
UNITED STATES OF AMERICA
BY T.F.H. PUBLICATIONS, INC.

Contents

CELSIUS° = 5/9 (F° − 32°)
FAHRENHEIT° = 9/5 C° + 32°
**METRIC MEASURES
AND EQUIVALENTS
CUSTOMARY U.S. MEASURES
AND EQUIVALENTS**

1 INCH (IN)		= 2.54 CM
1 FOOT (FT)	= 12 IN	= .3048 M
1 YARD (YD)	= 3 FT	.9144 M
1 MILE (MI)	= 1760 YD	= 1.6093 KM
1 NAUTICAL MILE	= 1.152 MI	= 1.853 KM

1 CUBIC INCH (IN³)		= 16.387 CM³
1 CUBIC FOOT (FT³)	= 1728 IN³	= .028 M³
1 CUBIC YARD (YD³)	= 27 FT³	= .7646 M³

1 FLUID OUNCE (FL OZ)		= 2.957 CL
1 LIQUID PINT (PT)	= 16 FL OZ	= .4732 L
1 LIQUID QUART (QT)	= 2 PT	= .946 L
1 GALLON (GAL)	= 4 QT	= 3.7853 L

1 DRY PINT		= .5506 L
1 BUSHEL (BU)	= 64 DRY PT	= 35.2381 L

1 OUNCE (OZ)	= 437.5 GRAINS	= 28.35 G
1 POUND (LB)	= 16 OZ	= .4536 KG
1 SHORT TON	= 2000 LB	= .9072 T
1 LONG TON	= 2240 LB	= 1.0161 T

1 SQUARE INCH (IN²)		= 6.4516 CM²	
1 SQUARE FOOT (FT²)	= 144 IN²	= .093 M²	
1 SQUARE YARD (YD²)		= 9 FT²	= .8361 M²
1 ACRE	= 4840 YD²	= 4046.86 M²	
1 SQUARE MILE(MI²)	= 640 ACRE	= 2.59 KM²	

Location, Design & Construction • 6

1 MILLIMETER (MM)		= .0394 IN
1 CENTIMETER (CM)	= 10 MM	= .3937 IN
1 METER (M)	= 1000 MM	= 1.0936 YD
1 KILOMETER (KM)	= 1000 M	= .6214 MI

1 SQ CENTIMETER (CM²)		= 100 MM²	= .155 IN²
1 SQ METER (M²)	= 10,000 CM²	= 1.196 YD²	
1 HECTARE (HA)	= 10,000 M²	= 2.4711 ACRES	
1 SQ KILOMETER (KM²)	= 100 HA	= .3861 MI²	

1 MILLIGRAM (MG)		= .0154 GRAIN
1 GRAM (G)	= 1000 MG	= .0353 OZ
1 KILOGRAM (KG)	= 1000 G	= 2.2046 LB
1 TONNE (T)	= 1000 KG	= 1.1023 SHORT TONS
1 TONNE		= .9842 LONG TON

1 CUBIC CENTIMETER (CM³)		= .061 IN³	
1 CUBIC DECIMETER (DM³)		= 1000 CM³	= .353 FT³
1 CUBIC METER (M³)		= 1000 DM³	= 1.3079 YD³
1 LITER (L)	= 1 DM³	= .2642 GAL	
1 HECTOLITER (HL)	= 100 L	= 2.8378 BU	

Selecting Stock • 35

The author is sincerely appreciative of the many photographic sources which have made this book possible. Especially helpful were Stapeley Water Gardens for all the pond photos, Dr. Herbert R. Axelrod, Zen Nippon Airinkai for all the koi photos, Fred Rosenzweig for many of the goldfish photos, Michael Gilroy, Ed Taylor, Mark Smith, Piednoir Aqua Press, Jorg Vierke, Lothar Wischnath, Burkhard Kahl, Roloff Beni and Dr. Denis Terver.

Looking at the history of fish ponds, we must inevitably start at the beginning, the keeping of fish as a food. Many of these ponds were natural bodies of water into which fish were introduced so that they would be on hand when needed. While in these ponds, some fish would inevitably breed and a resident population would become established. This was the start of fish farming. In Europe the Common Carp (*Cyprinus carpio*) was used to stock these ponds. This species originated in the area around the Black Sea and eastwards to Turkestan, but over the centuries it has spread far and wide. In China and the Far East, however, it was the ancestor of the Goldfish (*Carassius auratus*) which was more commonly

In periods of abundance hobbies develop and breeding ornamental fish is one of the more ancient ones.

Trying to track the history of the development of Goldfish and Koi is difficult because of the time scale we are looking at. We know for sure that there are records of colored fish as long ago as 265 AD being seen in the wild. What is not certain is whether these fish were Goldfish, Koi or some other cyprinid.

Proper domestication of Goldfish seems to have started during the Sung Dynasty which was about 1000 years ago, and during the Ming Dynasty (1368 - 1644) a great many variations of Goldfish were developed. But probably not all the types available today existed then because, as with all other

became widespread by the mid 1750's. By the end of the 1700's, Goldfish were all the rage amongst the English aristocracy. One of the main exponents was Horace Walpole, the Earl of Oxford, who was constantly giving Goldfish to his friends and acquaintances.

Modern Koi development has a more recent past. In the Niigata Prefecture region of Japan during the seventeenth century colored sports of Common Carp were selected to breed from. By selecting the different scaled and colored forms and breeding for these differences, many varieties were established.

Up until the beginning of the twentieth century, though, Koi were almost unknown outside this small region of Japan, but in 1914 some of the most beautiful varieties were exhibited in Tokyo and Crown Prince Hirohito was presented with some. From that moment on Koi became fashionable in Japan, and this soon spread to the rest of the world.

Originally artificial ponds had to be made from substances such as clay, which is difficult to work with and prone to leaking. Later came concrete which, with some skill and hard work, can make a very serviceable pond. But it was the development of laminated P.V.C. and synthetic rubber liners in England during the early 1960's which sparked off the current explosion in pond–keeping and water–gardening. Today many garden centres have a coldwater fish section and all the equipment needed to build your own pond. Many also stock

Common Goldfish are the best for an outdoor pond. This is *Carassius auratus*.

used as a food fish and even today Goldfish are a significant food fish in this area.

It is a relatively small step from the keeping of fish in a pond as food to keeping them for ornamental reasons. Basically, the difference stems from just how hungry you are.

living things, the Goldfish is a continually developing creature.

Goldfish–keeping as a hobby started in Europe as long ago as 1611, although later imports in 1691 and 1728 may have been the source of the fish which preformed fiber-glass ponds like the one my father installed all those years ago.

One of the recurring problems in man–made ponds is green water. This is caused by free–floating algae which feed on waste products produced by fish and other animals in the pond. In the past, most ponds would be afflicted at one time or another and even inclusion of artificial filtration and lots of growing plants only seemed to limit its development. One of the great discoveries of modern times, as far as pond keeping is concerned, is that, when green water passes over a source of ultraviolet

The common Carp, *Cyprinus carpio*, is the fish from which the Japanese colored carp (Koi) originated.

light the algae are killed. If it is strong enough, even any free-swimming fish parasites will also be destroyed, thus reducing the risk of parasitic infestation. At a stroke, permanently clear water was a possibility for the pond keeper, and the filter and pond manufacturers have been quick to develop this little gadget into an easy and relatively cheap form for home pond use.

The most popular fish for the garden pond are Japanese colored carp called Koi. There are many color varieties. From left to right, these champion fish are: hikari-mono, kinginrin, kohaku and bekko.

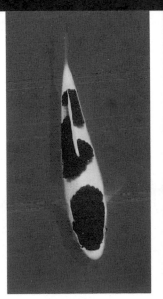

Location, Design & Construction

LOCATION

Choosing the correct location for your fish pond is of utmost importance if it is to be really successful. To begin with, if it is an ornamental pond, it will be a major feature of your garden and can add or detract a great deal from the appearance of the whole. Secondly, the well–being of the fish and plants also depends on the location. So what factors do we need to consider when deciding where to put a pond?

As far as the fish are concerned, the pond must be positioned where no harmful substances can fall into the water and poison them. Foremost amongst these are chemical sprays used on trees or plants near the pond. For this reason, make sure your pond is well away from the vegetable garden or fruit trees (unless you are an organic gardener) and do not use any chemicals on the plants around your pond. It is also worth giving a thought to the activities of your neighbors. Sprays have a habit of floating around on the air and someone treating a tree 30 ft. or more away can inadvertently poison your fish.

Other sources of problems can be the leaves, flowers, buds and other debris produced by overhanging trees. All parts of some trees, like Laburnum, are actively poisonous. Others, such as Willows and Poplars, have leaves which contain dangerous chemicals. Don't think that evergreens are any better in this respect; Holly and Laurel leaves are poisonous and are constantly shed by these evergreens. Even nonpoisonous overhanging trees will drop vast amounts of debris into a pond. This settles on the bottom and slowly rots producing noisome waste products which will harm your fish and discolor the water.

This Zen priest contemplating in the Daisen-in Daitokuji Temple, Kyoto, Japan, uses the Koi pond for serene peace.

The Koi pond at the Katsura Detached Palace in Kyoto, Japan. Choosing the correct location has a lot to do with the purposes for which you have designed your pond and the physical space available.

The plants in your pond will also be affected by the location. If it is a closed in, shady site your water lilies are unlikely to flower with any regularity or profusion. Other oxygenating plants will produce only limited growth which may upset the balance of your pond and encourage green algae.

When you take all these factors into consideration, it becomes clear an open sunny site is the ideal location for any pond. This should also be somewhere it can be viewed from the house and patio to enable you to get full enjoyment out of it.

You don't want your pond to be surrounded with trees. In the Fall of the year, the leaves drop into the water making it tan and very acid. This is the upper garden of the Shugakuin Rikyo in Kyoto.

Koi ponds can be very variable in design, as this magnificent water garden shows. It is the Stream Garden, Shugakuin Rikyo, Kyoto, Japan.

You will also need to give a thought to the services which are going to be needed to maintain your pond. If filtration, fountains or other water features are going to be included, then you will need access to electricity near by. For filling and topping up the pond, a water tap should be within reasonable distance. You must also have a hose long enough to reach from the tap to your pond. On one occasion I remember talking to an aquarist who planned to fill his new pond by bucket until it was pointed out he would have to make over 500 trips to even half fill it!

Another factor to take into consideration is that your pond will be like a magnet for friends and family, so a path of some sort will be needed. If one is already present in the garden it can save a lot of hard work if the pond is located by it.

Finally, you need to consider the type of garden soil in your garden. Most gardens have only one type of soil, but some have patches of clay or permanently boggy areas. My current home has a patch of clay soil plus a boggy area and I have avoided both when building my latest pond.

The reason for avoiding clay soil is obvious to anyone who has had to garden on this awful substance. My last house had a garden

where all the soil was heavy clay and it made gardening a chore rather than a pleasure. During dry weather it becomes as hard as iron and impossible to work, whilst during wet weather it becomes a sticky grunge which clogs everything up. Indeed, digging out the hole for a pond was such hard work I seriously considered giving up the project altogether. If you have no choice in the matter, and can afford it, hire a mechanical digger to do the job for you. Otherwise, check to ensure that your medical insurance is fully paid up!

Boggy soil presents other problems. You might be forgiven for thinking this would be the ideal place to have a pond but in actual fact it is the worst. During construction the hole will fill with water and make working

conditions very difficult. Trying to construct a concrete pond in these conditions is nearly impossible, and if you use a liner it may lift up with the pressure of water underneath.

A beautiful garden pond can be surrounded with terrestrial plants such as the *Polygonum dimity* shown here.

All this is based on the assumption that you are constructing a normal ornamental pond for your garden, but if you are planning to breed your fish then you would be well advised to have some small ponds for rearing the youngsters. Since these are utilitarian rather than ornamental, they can be tucked away in a quiet part of the garden well out of sight. In general, few plants will be incorporated in these so the amount of sunlight they receive will not be very important, but all the other points already mentioned should be taken into consideration.

DESIGN

The thought of designing your own pond can be a little daunting to start with, and I am sure this is the reason so many people opt for the prefabricated fibreglass ponds. In fact it can be a real opportunity to create something all of your own which is both beautiful and practical, providing that a few basic rules are followed.

these will have to be limited to marginal shelves in the pond or containers around the edges. This prevents the strong lines of a formal pond being broken up.

If you have decided on a pond in your lawn then it can be formal or informal and the deciding factor here will be the general planting of your garden. If you like your flower beds packed full of all differ-

Once you have decided on a formal or informal pond, you need to consider what kind of fish you are going to house in it. If you want Koi Carp then you are going to need as large a pond as possible. Remember, these fish grow very big and will need space if they are to do well in captivity. Personally, I would not consider housing these beautiful fish in any-

Stapeley Water Gardens display pond, courtesy of Stapeley Water Gardens, Limited.

First, you must consider the setting your pond is going to be seen in. If it is to be part of a patio or next to a wall, then a formal design is probably going to be the most suitable. By formal design all we really mean is a regular shape such as a square, rectangle, or circle. Plants can still be incorporated, but

ent kinds of plants along the cottage garden theme, an informal design to your pond will look more in keeping with the rest of the garden. If, on the other hand, you tend to plant your garden in formal lines or regular planting sequences, a more formal design for your pond will be needed.

thing under a 20 ft. x 10 ft. pond. Filtration will also need to be incorporated in a Koi pond, so think about where you are going to place this. It is worth deciding on which filtration system you are going to install before you have started to construct your pond. This way you know how big the unit is

An absolutely magnificent water garden created along the lines of a natural pond, with stepping stones instead of a bridge. This is at the Heian Shrine, Kyoto, Japan.

and how you are going to disguise or hide it before the pond is built.

Goldfish are smaller and much more accommodating, but even so, a pond with less than 30 sq. ft. of surface area is unlikely to be satisfactory for fish in the long run. Filtration is also an optional rather than an essential ingredient for a Goldfish pond, but it is still worth

particularly harsh climate you will have to go deeper than this. In some areas 3 ft. or even 3 ft. 6 inches may be needed. Koi ponds also require deeper water and these are usually constructed 4 to 5 ft. deep.

Safety is also important when designing a pond. A sunken pond without a built–up wall around it is a real hazard to both young and old

would have provided a refuge for them to climb out on if I had thought of it. My present pond has a bog garden attached to it which allows any animal which falls in the water an easy escape route.

When designing your pond you should remember to include some marginal shelves about 8 to 10 inches below the water's surface. This allows you enough depth

A beautiful display pond with a brightly colored bridge in the background, courtesy of Stapeley Water Gardens, Limited.

including even if it is just to prevent it looking like a stagnant green mire rather than a fish pond.

Apart from overall size, the depth of a pond is important. All ponds should have a minimum depth of 2 ft. in at least one area. This prevents the water from freezing solid in the winter and killing the fish. But if you live in a

alike. Small children can easily fall into a pond and drown if not properly supervised, and animals often fall victim to ponds which have no escape route. One of my early ponds had steep sides with nowhere for small animals to escape, and I regularly found dead hedgehogs and other small animals in it. Baskets containing marginal plants

for the deep water marginals to be located correctly, and by using bricks to raise the containers, shallow water marginals can also be made to feel comfortable.

When you have a clear idea of the size and shape of the pond you plan to construct, go out into the garden and mark out the rough outline on the ground. A piece of rope or

A scree garden composed of stones.

a hose can be used for this. Next, look at it from all sides and try to imagine what it will look like when it is complete. If you are satisfied, view it from inside the house; go upstairs and look at it from this perspective. Once you are sure you will be happy with the final look of the pond, you can start construction.

mechanical digger would also be useful, and will take a lot of the hard work out of digging the hole.

Apart from the hard work involved in digging the hole for your pond, there is really no great art in this part of the construction process. Giving some thought to where you are finally going to place the

other, then the final water level will reveal this and make the whole thing look very odd. Use a long piece of wood resting on each side and the spirit level placed in the middle of this to check.

BUILDING A CONCRETE POND
In the past, building a pond meant using concrete to

A lovely small water garden using a heron to keep other herons away from it. Herons are very territorial and their turf is usually respected by other herons.

CONSTRUCTION
Building a pond is a lot of hard work. All the digging, moving of soil, and other construction work will take it out of a fit young person and can cause serious health problems for the not so fit or older person. If at all possible, try to "volunteer", trap, or otherwise blackmail friends and relatives into helping you with the heavy work. Hiring a

huge pile of earth produced will save you some work. With one pond I built, I placed the soil on the patio until the pond was installed and then decided I wanted it at the other end of the garden thus doubling the amount of soil humping.

Make sure the edges of the pond's hole are level using a spirit level. If one side is higher than the

construct it, but today there are other and better choices available and I shall cover all of these in turn. First, we must consider concrete as a pond building material. One of its good points is its strength, but balancing this out is its inflexibility. With the stresses caused by expanding sheets of ice, soil subsidence, and shrinkage in dry weather, concrete ponds are very likely

A semi-risen water garden pond.

to crack. The risk of this happening can be reduced by proper design and construction, but in the end it is the inherent weakness of this material.

Another problem with concrete is the need to use wooden shuttering to hold the side walls in place while it is drying. This limits the shape to a square, rectangle or other simple design to allow you to build the shuttering. Hardboard can be used to create limited curves, so some informality can be introduced, but how successful you will be depends on your woodworking skills as much as anything else. The shuttering will need to be 4" smaller all around than the hole is.

If you do decide to make your pond out of concrete

then you need to dig the hole 5" larger all around and 10" deeper than the final pond size. This allows for the concrete and rendering thickness around the sides, plus 5" of hard-core, which will be used on the pond's bottom to help prevent subsidence. The sides must have about a 20 degree slope, so for every 3 inches you go down you need to go in 1 inch. This will help prevent ice from cracking the concrete. Remember to build your shuttering with a similar slope.

Marginal shelves can be constructed at this time by designing your shuttering to create a shelf about 10" below the water level and 1' wide. These shelves can be located at strategic points around the

pond, or a continuous one can be built at the same level all around the edge.

Once the hole is dug, you need to ram the hardboard into place. Apart from stones and rubble, include plenty of coarse gravel so that all the holes are filled in between the larger pieces of hardboard. Once this is done, you must make sure you have everything needed to construct your pond, and that the weather is set to be dry for the next few days.

To make up the concrete for 20 square feet of pond area (add the area of each side to the base area and if you are making any shelves at this time add their areas in as well) you will need 1 hundredweight of cement, 2 hundredweight of sharp sand, 4 hundredweight of coarse aggregate and 2 lbs. of water-proofing powder.

To start, you will only need to make up enough concrete to cover the base with a two inch layer so keep this in mind when mixing each batch. Add the correct amount of waterproofing

Now take a break for an hour. This allows the concrete to set sufficiently for you to lower the shuttering on it. Next fill in the 4" gap between the shuttering and the hole with concrete. This should be done as quickly as possible and completed in a few hours.

buckets of sharp sand, with waterproofing powder added at the rate of 5 lb per cwt of cement used. Once again, mix this dry and then add water to make a stiff paste. This is then used to coat all surfaces with a 1 inch thick layer. Try to have the next batch being mixed up whilst you are applying the first (your 'volunteers' can help here).

Once dry, it can be painted with a pond sealant to prevent lime from leaching out into the water and killing fish and plants, or alternatively the pond can be filled with water and allowed to stand for a week. It is then emptied and refilled. This procedure is repeated every week for 6 weeks before it is finally filled with water permanently.

A lovely water garden.

powder to a bucket of cement. Place this in the mixer and add two buckets of sharp sand and three buckets of aggregate. Mix all the ingredients carefully before adding water until a stiff paste has been created. Be careful not to add too much water all at once. A little at a time is the best way with this. When you have finished, the paste should be still stiff enough to cut into slices. This can now be poured on the base and the next batch made up. Keep going until your have your 2" thick layer on the bottom, at which time you need to add a reinforcing steel mesh or chicken wire over the bottom. Once in place, continue adding concrete until this is 2" deep above the mesh.

If you are building a particularly large pond, you may be forced to work in stages because you need to walk on the base to install the shuttering. In this case, leave the base to set for a day or two and make sure you rough–up the edges so that it will properly join the concrete walls which will be added later.

Once the basic shell has been completed, you will need to leave it to set until you can safely remove the shuttering and walk on the base. This may take only a day or it may be several depending on weather conditions. However long it takes, you should add the rendering as soon as possible.

The rendering is made of two buckets of cement to six

INSTALLING A PREFABRICATED POND.

Installing a prefabricated pond is the easiest method of having a pond in the garden. There is a huge range of designs available although some are too small or too shallow to make adequate permanent ponds for fish (though they are fine for quarantine or rearing purposes). If you stick to the guidelines suggested in the design section, you will be able to purchase a perfectly serviceable prefabricated pond.

When digging the hole for a prefabricated pond, make it a little larger than the actual pond and firm down the base as much as possible. Position the pond in its hole and check that it is level using a piece of wood resting across tile edges and a spirit level. Make sure it is level each way and then start to backfill the soil. Take special care to pack it under each of the marginal shelves and press it down firmly all around the edges. The edges can then be finished off using paving stones, rockwork, or turf and without further ado your pond can be filled with water.

INSTALLING A POND LINER

Pond liners are a little more tricky to install than prefabricated ponds, but you can determine the size, shape and depth yourself and they tend to produce a more natural looking effect in the end. There are several different materials on the market, but by far and away the best is butyl rubber. This has a life expectancy of 50 to 100 years and is very durable. Laminated PVC can also be used but this has a shorter life expectancy although it is cheaper.

You can calculate the size of liner you need for your pond by simply measuring its maximum overall length and width and adding on twice the maximum depth. So a kidney–shaped pond which has a maximum length of one inch and width of 6' with its maximum depth being 3' will need a liner 16' by 12'.

With this type of pond you must remember that the hole you are digging is going to be the final shape of your pond, so make sure the walls slope at a 20 degree angle from the vertical and remember to include any marginal shelves you want. These need to be 1' wide and 10" below the final water depth. If the pond is to be finished off with paving stones which are laid flush with the surroundings, then the area around the pond must be dug to a depth of 2".

Once the hole is dug you must carefully examine the bottom and sides, removing any sharp stones or objects.

A pre-fabricated water garden sunk into the ground.

Next cover the base and marginal shelves with sand, sifted soil, sawdust, old polythene, or anything else which will produce a smooth soft surface to protect the liner. I have used old carpets, underfelt, newspapers, and fertilizer sacks for this job in the past. All produced good results and cost nothing.

Once your hole has been prepared, you should spread the liner out over the top. Put weights like stones or bricks all around but allow the centre to sag into the hole a little. Next start filling the liner with water. As it fills, the liner will stretch and fill the hole but some of the weights can be removed to allow some inward movement as well. The stretching properties of this type of liner will reduce any creasing but only if the liner is kept fairly taut during filling. Once full, remove all the other weights and trim off any surplus liner to about 6" from the edge.

To finish the edge, either use paving stones, rocks, turf or some other plant life. If you use paving stones these must be long enough to project 2" over the pond edge and still have enough stone to be stable. These should be bedded on a mixture of 1 part cement and 3 parts sand made into a stiff paste. Make sure the stones are level and make sure none of the mixture falls into the water. If just a little falls in, it can be

removed without any risk but a lot falling in will leach lime into the water and kill the fish. To prevent this from happening the pond will have to be emptied and refilled after it has been cleaned.

If plants are being used to cover the edge, then the surplus liner will need to be buried in the soil and plants or turf laid over the top. Since rooting may be shallow in this area, choose low growing spreading plants which will spread to cover all the edge. Turf can be laid right down to the waters edge.

BREEDING AND REARING PONDS

These are constructed in any of the three methods already outlined, but they are generally much smaller and are only in temporary use. For this reason they can be shallower than a permanent pond, about 1' is deep enough, and should be constructed in such a way that they can be easily drained for cleaning. The best ponds of this type I have seen, have all been raised above ground level, and some of the cheapest and easiest to use have been childrens' paddling pools. These are usually just the right size and can easily be emptied out and cleaned at the end of the year. This type of pool can also be used to quarantine new fish, which is vital to protect your established fish from disease.

Small containers can be converted to water gardens provided they don't leak and are not toxic.

Find an old barrel, cut it in half, and you have yourself a very charming water garden.

An enchanting waterfall found in Kenrokuen Park's Koi pond, Kanazawa, Japan.

Water Features

Fish really appreciate moving water in their ponds. It helps increase the amount of oxygen in water and provides a current for fish to swim against, both beneficial side effects of including a fountain or waterfall within your pond.

FOUNTAINS

Of the two, a fountain is easiest to install and there are many readymade setups you can buy from your local garden centre or aquatic outlet. These range from a simple vertical jet of water coming out of a spout attached to the water pump right up to elaborate statues with multiple jets of water surging out of the mouths of various cherubs, etc. The style you choose will depend very much on personal taste and the type of environment it will be a feature of. The more elaborate statues, particularly of classical design, look best in a formal setting, whereas small simple statues or water jets look good in an informal setting.

One factor to consider when selecting a fountain for your pond is how high any jet will spray. High jets look very spectacular but on a windy day so much water will blow away that your pond may soon be in danger of being drained. Another side effect of high jets is the increase in evaporation. A pond may lose as much as 5% of its water volume in a single day because of a water jet. Obviously

this will have to be corrected quickly or marginal plants will soon be sitting above the water line and may die.

One type of fountain which I have never seen for sale and which looks particularly good in an informal pond is a cobble fountain. To make one of those, all you have to do is position your water pump

A proper water garden requires a fountain to aerate the water.

where you want to have your fountain and attach a piece of hose to the outlet. Now build an island of cobbles by the side or over your water pump, threading the nose up through the middle of the cobbles. When the island is high enough, cut off the surplus hose and attach a spray or jet nozzle to the end. Alternatively, leave the hose end as it is which will make the fountain look like a bubbling up spring. Bog plants can be fitted between

the cobbles in pots which will add to the natural look of the feature.

WATERFALLS

Waterfalls have been commonly associated with ponds since the first person who dug a pond wondered what to do with that huge pile of soil. A rockery immediately sprang to mind and then a mini stream with a waterfall or series of waterfalls. Today it is possible to buy readymade molded fibreglass or plastic pieces which can be fitted together to make a series of cascades. These are cheap and relatively easy to position, but look very artificial. Making your own waterfall is not too difficult and the effect can be much more natural.

First of all, you will need some pond liner (leftover pieces from the main pond are

Vallerie Hersch sits atop the waterfall she and her husband built on their estate.

usually enough for this, although if you want a large top pond you will have to buy a liner of the correct size) and a water pump which can pump the water to the top of the waterfall. Some cheap pumps have a high turnover but little power, and cannot pump water more than a few inches above the water's surface, so check this out before buying.

Next arrange the soil pile in the shape you want. If it is going to be a rockery, incorporate most of the stones at this time but make sure you leave enough room for the water channel. One of the common problems with this sort of construction is soil from the hill tends to be washed into the lower pond by rain, so make sure you keep the slope gentle and everything stable. The hose from your water pump or filter must be buried in the ground at this stage with the outlet just by the top of the ministream or the edge of the top pond.

Now you need to fit the liner in position. If you are having a top pond then the hole should be prepared in the same way as for the main pond. Any cascades or waterfalls should be preceded by a small pond area with the water held back by an inch or two high lip. This is created under the liner by piling soil up. A catchment pond below the drop should also be included but this can be made by digging a small hole. The liner must come about 4 inches above the water course on each side and the edges can be covered with the same kind of rock used for the rockery. The lip of each waterfall can be covered with

Two square bubble fountain water gardens.

stones or pieces of wood to disguise the pond liner.

Finally the liner can be covered with gravel or small pebbles or left open if you want. Once complete, the waterfall should be turned on and carefully watched for a few hours. During this time, make sure everything is stable and water is not seeping over the edges. This is another way to empty your pond very quickly and it is best to find

any problems before they become serious.

One of the side effects of a waterfall, besides increasing the water's oxygen content, is the additional filtration effect it has. Bacteria grow on all the submerged surfaces and help filter the water. This can have a very beneficial effect on the fishes' well-being, but it must be kept running all the time for this to really build up.

The famous Gan Aquarium Fish Farm in Singapore developed this Yellow Snakeskin Guppy, which they grow outdoors in their tropical water gardens.

OTHER WATER FEATURES

In recent years half barrels and other containers have been used to make small water features for the patio. These can be very attractive and may include fountains and growing plants, but most are too small for Goldfish and Koi to live in and have largely been ignored by aquarists. There are, however, some species of fish which will live very happily in these small containers during the summer months. For this reason I have decided to include how to make a half barrel into a mini pond for the patio.

First of all hunt up a barrel or half barrel. These days many of these are being sold in garden centres as plant containers, so you should not have too much trouble finding one. If the bottom has a hole drilled in it you will have to line it, but if you are lucky and can find one without a hole then you can use it as it is. Either way make sure it is

Gambusia, the original mosquito fish, is ideal for ponds because it eats mosquito larvae.

Heterandria formosa, a small mosquito fish, is helpful but it cannot tolerate frozen water.

thoroughly cleaned out and scrubbed over. Remove any nails or sharp pieces of wood sticking out inside and position it where it will remain permanently.

If you are lining it, then you need to cover inside with a layer of wet newspapers or old carpet. Next fit your liner loosely into the barrel and start to fill it. Keep the liner taut as it fills to reduce the amount of wrinkles which form. Once full, cut off the surplus liner and water pressure will keep the liner in place.

If you are not lining your barrel you can start to fill it once the cleaning process is complete. Take particular care over the cleaning since anything left behind will pollute the water and may kill anything you put in the barrel.

Once full, leave it standing for a couple of days to allow any chlorine to dissipate or add a water conditioner if you have chloramine in your tapwater. Now add a small water lily (this is one which only grows to a small maximum size rather than a small sized normal water lily), tropical lilies are very good for this. A small pot of submerged water plants should also be included and possibly some marginals or trailers growing in pots attached around the rim.

Once all is in place you can add some fish. *Gambusia holbrooki, Heterandria formosa* or Guppies make good additions to this type of water feature. Some of the tougher species of North American killifish can also be used or Mexican goodeids. All of these fish can only be put in the barrel once all risk of frost has passed and must be removed in the fall before the frosts start. The tropical water lily must also be moved to a protected environment for the winter months.

Above the ground water gardens become colder than sunken ones, but they are safer for children and pets.

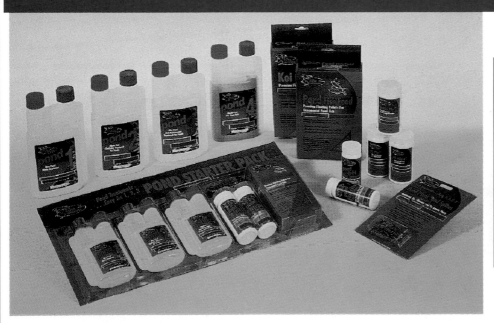

A variety of water treatment and related products is available to care for fish and aquatic plants in backyard ponds or water gardens. Photo courtesy of Henri Water Gardening™ from Mardel Laboratories, Inc.™

Filtration & Pond Maintenance

FILTRATION

The key to successful fish keeping is knowing how to maintain a healthy balance. Fish produce wastes in the form of ammonia which will build up in the water and eventually reach poisonous levels. In a natural pond *Nitrosomonas* bacteria break the poisonous ammonia down into nitrites. These are in turn broken down by bacteria of the genus *Nitrobacter* into what are only mildly toxic nitrates used by plants and algae as food.

All this happens to a certain extent in any fish tank or artificial pond, but problems arise when too much ammonia is produced by the fish for the natural system to cope with. This happens in a newly set up pond and is the reason why it is important to only introduce a few fish to a pond or tank initially—so the bacteria have enough time to become properly established. Later, when more fish are added, the bacteria can cope with the increased waste

production (up to a point, of course).

Ammonia poisoning will also occur when too many fish are kept in a pond. They produce too much waste for the natural system to cope with, so ammonia builds up and kills the fish. This can be prevented by keeping stocking levels down to those recommended for each species or by including artificial filtration.

Filtration is split into three types: biological, chemical and mechanical. Of these, biological filtration is the most important for pondkeepers. This form of filtration makes use of the natural nitrogen cycle already described but gives it a helping hand by providing ideal conditions for the nitrifying bacteria to live in.

These bacteria need a good supply of oxygen and a suitable surface to live on. This is provided by pushing oxygenated pond water over something with a very large surface area. Sponge–like pads are sometimes used, but small balls, brushes, large pea gravel, or even hair curlers have been employed for this purpose. As the water passes over these surfaces the bacteria living on them break down the ammonia and nitrites into nitrates which are then returned to the pond.

Under normal circumstances, growing aquatic plants will absorb these nitrates and use them for food. Unfortunately, in many ponds there are not enough plants growing to use up all the food so single–celled algae

The moss garden at the Saihoji Temple, Kyoto, Japan. Natural ponds like this require professional maintenance.

This place is called Green Hell, Beppu, Japan. The mornings are very cold, the pond is watered via a hot spring and this causes the continuous steam.

Every pond needs essentials such as foods, natural treatments and maintenance items. Your local pet shop usually carries these items. Photo courtesy of HBH Aquarium Products. Call them at 1-800-766-FISH to find the dealer nearest you.

start to reproduce in large numbers and the water turns green.

Green water has been the bane of fishkeepers' lives ever since people started keeping ornamental fish. Not because it does any harm to fish, but because it prevents you from seeing them properly. Recently, however, it was discovered that passing green water over an ultra violet light source would kill the algae and ponds could be kept crystal clear. U.V. filters are now readily available and reasonably cheap. Many of the large pond filters include one within the unit which makes them even cheaper and easier to include in a pond setup. U.V. lamps have a limited effective life of only a year or two, so a replacement bulb will have to be purchased whenever the water starts to go green again.

Chemical filtration has only limited application as far as ponds are concerned. Activated carbon can be included in a filter system to absorb various waste products. This only has a very limited life and must be replaced with great frequency. It does, however, have a use when medication has been added to a pond because it will absorb the chemicals after they have affected treatment. Obviously this cannot be in use whilst the fish are being treated, but should be added to the filter unit afterwards.

One other chemical which has been used in chemical filtration is zeolite. This substance absorbs ammonia from water and can be very useful with a temporary quarantine or breeding pond where a large biological filter

Ultra-violet germicidal energy is superior for killing algae, bacteria and protozoa exposed to its rays. It can keep any water garden crystal clear when properly used. Photo courtesy of Emperor Aquatics. Call them at (610)970-0440 to locate the dealer nearest you.

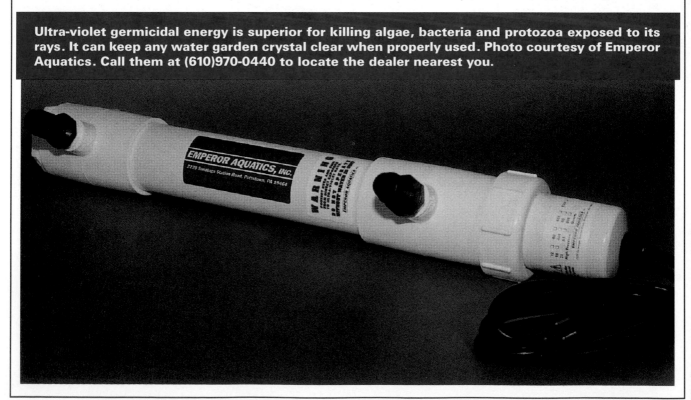

might be inappropriate. It will remove only a finite amount of ammonia before needing recharging. This is done by running it through a 10 % salt solution, after which it is rinsed well and returned to the filter unit.

Mechanical filtration is used in all commercially produced filters to remove particulate matter suspended in the water. Koi ponds tend to suffer from this more than Goldfish ponds because Koi love nothing better than to rummage through the substrate looking for tasty morsels to eat. The problem with this is the constant stirring action which blows large amounts of mulm and other debris into the water. Most filters have a sponge filter either on the front of the intake pipe or in the first compartment of the filter unit. This traps the debris and prevents it from entering the other filter chambers. The sponge filter must, however, be regularly cleaned or the flow of water through the filter

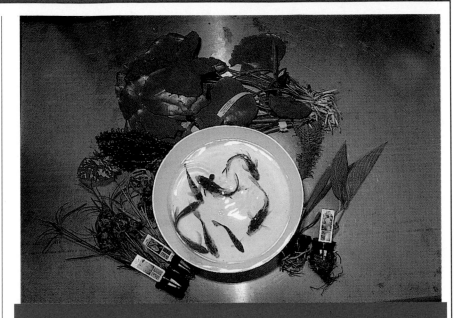

Water lilies, marginal plants and live pond fish are available year-round from Professional Aquarist. Call (941) 543-5300 for more information.

will be reduced and its efficiency compromised.

Even with good filtration, nitrates are going to build up in a pond if there are not enough growing plants to make use of them as a food. For this reason, it is a good idea to change about 10% of the water in your pond every month. This will dilute the nitrate content down and give the fish a blast of fresh water which they will appreciate. If you live in a water area where chloramines are added to the tap water, you will have to add a water conditioner to the fresh water. In other areas, unless very high levels of chlorine are used in your water supply, you should not need to add any chemical during such a small water change.

A YEAR IN THE LIFE OF A POND

Pond maintenance and how you feed your fish will depend upon the time of the year and the water temperature. For this reason it makes sense to look at the pond during each of the seasons and summarise the jobs which should be done at that time and how the fish should be looked after.

Spring

Spring is a lovely time in both the garden and the pond.

Koi require special food. They should NOT be fed regular aquarium fish food pellets. Photo courtesy of O.S.I. Koi Food.

At this time of year your fish have just come out of their winter hibernation and the temptation is to throw handfuls of food in to fatten them up. The danger with this is that their digestive systems have not started to function fully yet. It is best to wait until the water temperature is up to 55°F before starting to feed your fish every day. Up until that time just offer a little food when the fish can be seen swimming about near the surface on a particularly warm spring day. Initially Koi should be fed foods which are vegetable-based rather than having animal proteins in them. These should only be fed when the fish are fully active and feeding daily.

Spring is the time when diseases and other problems are most likely to break out in your fish. This is because their immune systems are still coming out of their winter dormancy and the animals are most at risk from infection. For this reason, a close watch should be kept on them and if you suspect any problems, net the affected fish out and have a close look at it.

Other jobs which need doing at this time of the year are cleaning out the filter and checking all the pipes and connectors for leaks. Submerged and marginal plants should be lifted and divided. If new fish are to be acquired during the coming season, then a quarantine pond or tank will have to be set up.

Apart from green water, one other alga causes pond keepers some problems. This is blanket weed. Unlike single celled free floating algae which U.V. sterilizers destroy, blanket weed attaches itself to

The biggest problem with water gardening is the uncontrollable growth of algae. This algae turns the pond into *pea soup*. With the use of a proper U.V. filter the algae problem is history.

a firm object and grows in long unsightly threads. During spring and summer, growth can be rapid and all encompassing. To reduce this pest you need as much plant life in the pond as possible and a long stick with a few nails hammered into it. This is pushed into a clump of the weed and twisted around until the algae is firmly entangled. Stick and algae are now pulled out of the pond. By repeating this process all around your pond you will soon remove the bulk of this pest. This needs to be done at least every two weeks during the spring and summer months. With a liner pond, great care needs to be taken with this chore because one false move can puncture the liner.

Summer

By now your fish should be fully active and may even be spawning from time to time. They should be fed twice a day now, but only as much as they can eat in 5 minutes. Many people over-feed their fish and pollute the water. I have never seen fish which have been starved to death but I have seen hundreds killed by polluted water. Always err on the cautious side and under-feed rather than over-feed. When you go away on holiday *do not get your neighbor to feed the fish*. Inexperienced people almost always over-feed fish and inadvertently pollute the water, killing the fish. Unless you are going away for more than 3 weeks, just leave them alone and they will come through your absence fine. If you are going away for longer than this then you will have to show an interested neighbor how to feed your fish properly. Do this several weeks before you go to be sure they have the hang of it.

Early summer is the best time to purchase any new fish and plants. They will have many months to settle down in their new environment, and most importers will have just brought in their new stock for sale. Remember to quarantine all new fish for 21 days before you give them a final check over and release them into the pond.

New plants should also be quarantined before introduction. This is because they may have been kept in a pond with diseased fish and still be harboring disease agents. Fourteen days will be long enough to kill most diseases and a final rinse under the tap should prevent anything still attached to them from getting into your pond.

If the amount of debris on the bottom of the pond has built up too much, then now is the time to give a pond a complete clean out. Turn off

settle down. If no temporary pond is available, keep the fish in covered buckets or other containers out of direct sunlight and place wet newspapers over the plants to keep them moist. Return fish and plants a couple of hours after

good idea to cover the pond with a fine meshed net to stop them falling on the water.

Remove any dead leaves from marsh plants and reduce the number of submerged oxygenators like *Elodea canadensis* and floating

This magnificent water garden is highlighted by a beautiful waterfall. It pays to invest in a natural-looking waterfall.

the filtration and remove the fish and plants to a temporary pond. The main pond can now be emptied and any mulm and other accumulated filth should be scooped out. Refill with fresh tapwater and use a water conditioner to make the water safe. Return the plants the next day and add the fish a day or two later once everything has had a chance to

the water conditioner has been added.

Autumn
Autumn is in many ways the most important time of the year for the pond owner. Any dead leaves and other debris have to be removed from the pond. If any trees are shedding lots of leaves nearby, then it might be a

plants like Water Soldiers. These always seem to multiply during the summer months and can overrun a pond if some are not removed each year. If you have tender plants like Water Hyacinths or Water Lettuce floating on top of your pond, these must be removed before the first frost. Otherwise they fall to pieces and start to rot in a few hours.

As temperatures fall, your fish will become more sluggish and tend to spend their time near the bottom. On warm days small feeds can still be offered but do this later in the day when the fish can be seen to be active near the surface. Make sure your fish are still feeding at this time and stop feeding altogether when regular nightly frosts occur. Koi must be back on a vegetable–based diet at this time of year.

Winter

The big worries during winter are ice and snow. Many pondkeepers think their fish are going to be frozen solid and die yet the nature of freshwater is such that this risk is reduced if the pond is deep enough. When water freezes it forms a crystal called ice which is less dense than the liquid form of the same substance. This means it floats and eventually covers the entire surface. This surface ice has an insulating effect and helps prevent the water below it freezing any more. So unless the temperature is very low for long

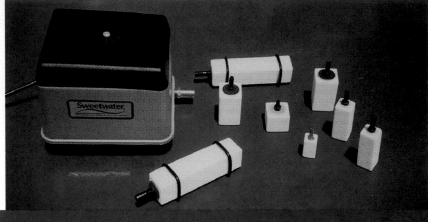

Air compressors provide the necessary air output and pressure to allow air diffusers to release air bubbles into the pond water, thereby circulating and aerating the water. Contact Aquatic Eco-Systems, Inc. at 1-800-422-3939 for the name of the pet shop nearest you selling these products.

periods, nothing more than a few inches of ice will develop on a pond and the fish will be safe and sound hibernating on the bottom. In some areas where the climate is very harsh water will freeze to a depth of several feet, and in these areas you will have to dig your pond deeper to protect the fish.

Another effect of ice is to close off the surface to gaseous exchange. Provided there is no rotting vegetation or other matter in the pond this will not cause too much of a

problem. It is, however, a good idea to melt a small hole in the surface and remove some of the water to create an air pocket below the ice. The hole is then covered with a piece of sacking to keep it open.

Pond heaters are on sale in most garden centres, and for people living in very cold areas with a reasonable budget to spend on their pond, purchasing one of these might be a good idea. It is not supposed to keep the pond ice free but just one small area of it to allow gaseous exchange. Most are low wattage so are not too expensive to run.

Snow on the other hand causes a problem of a different kind. Plants need light to photosynthesize and a thick layer of snow over a pond will block out the light. If this is left for days on end all the plants will die and start to rot, killing your fish. This is the most common cause of "winter kill" and yet it is so easy to remedy. Take a broom and sweep off the snow once a day.

Celestial Goldfish are active even when ice forms on the pond, must be fed during the winter. Koi are inactive when the water temperature drops below 50°F. and feeding them is not necessary.

Stocking Levels

The number of fish a pond can house will depend on its surface area. This is because it is at the surface that oxygen is absorbed by water and carbon dioxide is released. If there are too many fish in tne pond or they are too big, then they give off more carbon dioxide than the water can release into the atmosphere and soon start to suffer. In extreme cases they will die.

Filtration and the oxygenating effect it has on water will increase the amount of fish a body of water can hold. During power failures and other emergencies, however, the filter will cease to function and you can lose all your fish in a matter of just a few hours. For this reason, whilst good filtration is of benefit to your fish, you have to ignore it when calculating how many fish you can have in your pond.

Personally, to be on the safe side, I would have no more than 1inch of a fish's body length for every 24 sq. inches of surface area. This figure will need to be down-graded to 30 sq. inches if you are subjected to long periods of high temperatures during tne summer months.

To calculate a pond's surface area, multiply its length by its width. So a pond 10 ft. by 5 ft. (120 inches X 60 inches) has 7200 sq. inches of surface area and can hold 300 inches of fish. An 'L' shaped pond should be treated as two rectangles and the surface areas added together.

Above: Without aeration in the form of a waterfall, fountain or airstone, water gardens should not be overstocked with fishes. A suggested formula is one inch of fish length for every 24 square inches of water surface. This pond is overladen with plants and such dense planting is dangerous for pond fishes.

Below: A dangerous situation occurs when water is allowed to trickle down rocks which are dirty from accumulated dusty residues. The bubbles are danger signs.

Circular ponds are a little more difficult. Measure the diameter (the distance across the widest part) and halve it. Then multiply this figure by itself and multiply the total by 3.142. So a pond 20 ft. (240 inches) across will have a surface area of : 120 x 120 x 3.142 = 45244.8 sq. inches. This means it can hold up to 1885.2 inches of fish.

Oval ponds are treated in much the same way but you need to measure the width and length. These two figures are added together and divided by two. Now use this answer as if it were the diameter of a circular pond. So for an oval pond 10 ft. x 5 ft. (120 inches x 60 inches) we have: 120 + 60 = 180; 180/2 = 90 & 90/2 = 45; 45 X 45 X 3.142 = 6362.55 sq. inches or 265 inches of fish.

This is not the end of the story, however, because it is not just now you have to worry about, but the future. If you put 265 1" long fish into this oval pond, which according to the calculations it should be able to cope with, by the end of the season they will have grown and will be overburdening the system. So you have to take into account the adult size each fish will reach and work on that, rather than the actual size each fish is when you acquire it.

A magnificent Stapeley Water Gardens pond with clumps of lilies and *Iris* in the foreground.

Selecting Stock

Selecting healthy vibrant stock is one of the most important jobs you have to do when starting out with a new pond. Relying on the staff at the place at which you buy your fish may seem like a good idea, but in reality not all personnel are equally knowledgeable.

Dead or dying fish left in the tanks or ponds are one sure warning sign that the people selling them might not know how to care for them. In any dealer's tanks the odd fish will die (usually just as a customer walks in the door) but having significant numbers of dead fish or bodies left rotting in the setup means you should look elsewhere for your stock.

If all appears well on the surface, take a close look at the fish for sale. Fish which are thin and wasted or hanging around in a listless fashion with their fins clamped must be avoided. A dull white bloom which appears in patches on the surface of the body or cotton wool–like tufts are signs of fungus, whilst small white spots on the body and fins are usually parasites like White Spot. Fish with thread–like pieces hanging from any part of their body or with blood spots, or badly torn and damaged fins, plus any animal with an ulcer on the body, are also trouble. Keep well clear of any fish like these, and also do not buy any fish from the tanks or ponds which contain these sick animals.

Look for those fish which are swimming in a sprightly fashion with their fins open and well spread. Healthy fish are aware of your presence and will either swim towards you looking for food or away from you in fright. If they take no notice of you whatsoever they may be in the early stages of an illness and are best left where they are.

The rear end of this pond is fenced off for the quarantining of new fishes. Parasites, however, can leave the host fish and make their way into the pond proper, so this sort of quarantine is not very effective, but it is better than nothing. If fish break down with a bacterial infection, they can easily be captured and treated.

When you are satisfied with what you see, pick out the fish you want. If you are buying them from a pond, have them placed in a small tank or polythene bag and take a close look at them from all sides. This will be your first really good look at these fish and it will be your only chance to reject substandard animals. Do not be afraid of saying no to the sales assistant even at this stage and if he/she tries to talk you into taking it despite your misgiv-

ings, stick to your guns and refuse.

If you are planning to breed a particular variety of Goldfish or Koi, you might have to go to a private breeder for your initial stock. This is because the breeder will be working with inbred lines which have been established over many years. These fish are much more likely to produce a reasonable percentage of offspring which have the desired characteristics. Using two unrelated or distantly related fish purchased from normal trade sources may produce some good quality fish, but it is more likely to produce only relatively few having the correct combination of characteristics.

QUARANTINING NEW STOCK

All new fish you purchase must be properly quarantined

Stapeley Water Gardens sells fish and plants to the public. Their displays are suggestive of water gardens their clients can achieve and they have many visitors coming to their gardens for ideas they can apply to their own situations.

before they go into your pond. Any number of diseases can be introduced to your pond if you fail to quarantine new fish.

This should be done in an indoor aquarium or small pool outside. Aquaria are better because you can observe the fish more closely, but with large fish or if you have limited space, outdoor pools will have to be used. Tanks should have some form of filtration in them and regular partial water changes must be undertaken in both tanks and outdoor pools. Although these are only temporary quarters, the fishes' health will depend on good water quality.

During the quarantine period, the fish must be closely observed for diseases every day. The sooner any trouble is spotted the more likely you are to be able to successfully treat the animal concerned. If you do spot trouble, make sure you know for certain what the disease is before you attempt any treatment. More fish are killed through incorrect medical treatments and overdoses than through diseases themselves. If you are unsure of a diagnosis, take the affected fish to a vet for proper diagnosis and treatment.

The quarantine period should last at least 2 weeks and personally I prefer to keep a check on new fish for a month before putting them in my pond. This way I am sure no disease or parasite problem is going to make its way into my pond, and it gives me a chance to feed the new arrivals so they are in peak condition.

Koi

Over the centuries Koi have been developed into a wide range of color types and scalation. These are known today by their untranslated Japanese names, which gives them an exotic sound. However, many are nothing more than descriptions of the fishes' color or scalation.

During the early 1900's in Germany, fishes with a reduced number of scales were bred. These found their way over to Japan where they were crossed with Japanese Koi to produce Doitsu Koi. They have a few large scales, often in a different color to the rest of the body, and set in rows from behind the head to the caudal peduncle. In some varieties, this trait was enhanced until no scales were present and these are known as Leather Koi.

During the early 1980's in America, some long–finned hybrid carp turned up in a shipment. These were crossed into normal Koi and long–finned Butterfly Koi were produced. These are gaining in popularity all the time, but so far the range of colors is limited. Given time, the full range of Koi colors should be achievable.

The following is a list of the major color varieties available, although there are many subdivisions within each variety.

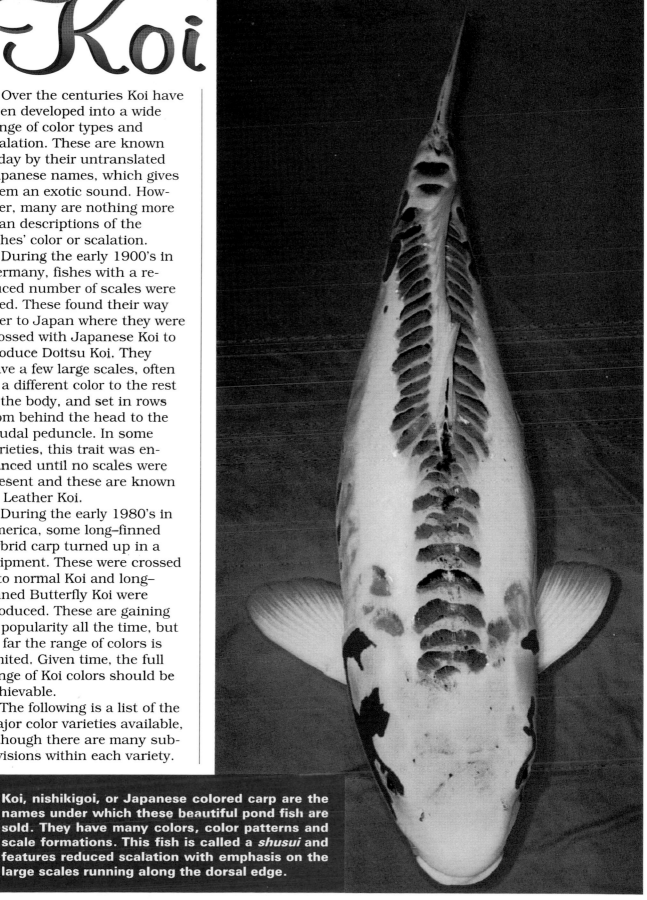

Koi, nishikigoi, or Japanese colored carp are the names under which these beautiful pond fish are sold. They have many colors, color patterns and scale formations. This fish is called a *shusui* and features reduced scalation with emphasis on the large scales running along the dorsal edge.

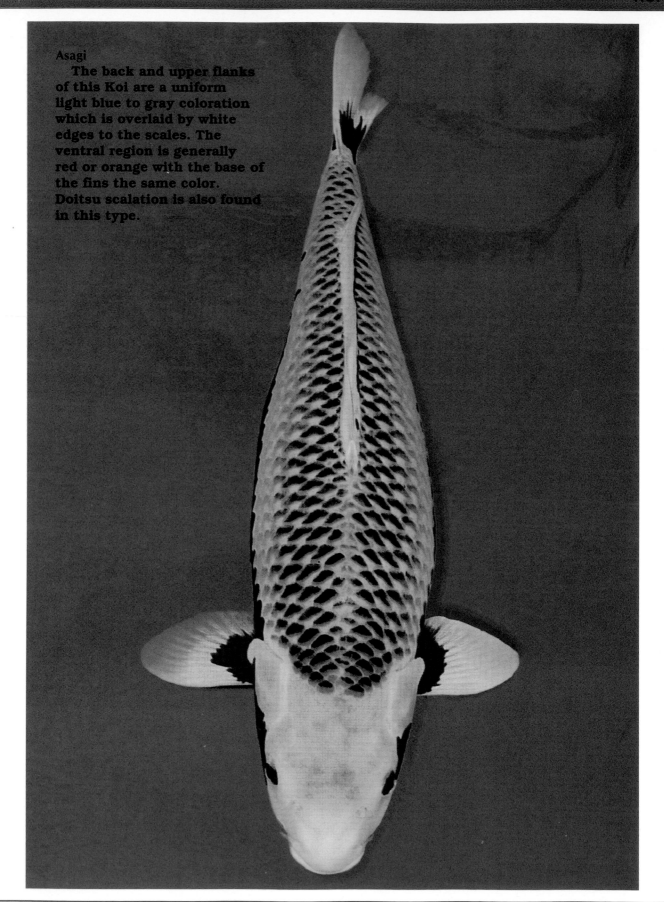

Asagi

The back and upper flanks of this Koi are a uniform light blue to gray coloration which is overlaid by white edges to the scales. The ventral region is generally red or orange with the base of the fins the same color. Doitsu scalation is also found in this type.

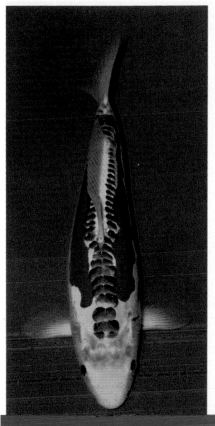

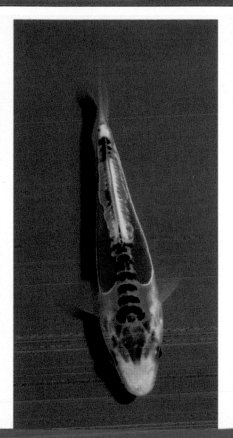

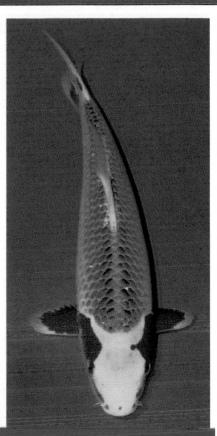

Six examples of champion Asagi-shusui koi with normal scalation and Doitsu (German) scalation. The Doitsu scales are huge and run along the dorsal edge and sides of the fish. Leather carp are also like Doitsu with abnormal scales and scale patterns.

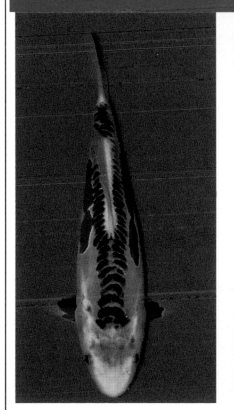

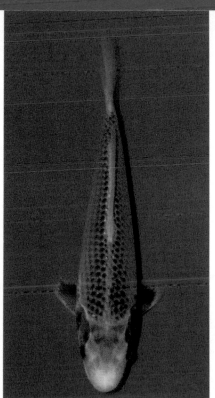

Bekko
These are basically single–colored fish with an overlay of black. They come in red, orange, yellow and white forms and the black scales should be limited to the back of the fish. Leather and Doitsu forms are available.

Six champion quality Bekko. The center fish above has metallic scales which further enhance its beauty.

Kawarimono
This group includes a whole range of varieties which do not fit in with the other types. The highly popular Goshiki Koi come into this group.

Six champion Kawarimono. These fish are beautiful but they do not fit the standards of any of the categories recognized by the Japanese Koi authorities, so they are dumped into the Kawarimono section in Koi shows.

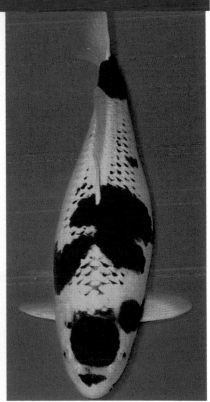

Kohaku
This is the most popular Koi variety both in the West and in Japan. The body is white with red patches of varying sizes and shapes depending on the specific variety. Good quality specimens have only pure white and brilliant red colors. A yellowish tinge to the white is a fault, as are black markings anywhere on the fish. Scaling can be either normal or Doitsu.

Koi are, with rare exceptions, only viewed from above when they are kept in water gardens. Thus the color patterns visible from above are what count. The Kohaku patterns are the bases of fantasies...they look like steps, maps, lightning, or whatever the judge or owner happens to feel. This characteristic makes the Kohaku the most popular color variety of ornamental Koi.

Kinginrin
   Another group of Koi with a metallic sheen, but this one has many silver markings on the body. There are lots of variations in this type, but Kinginrin Sanke (three-colors) are one of the more commonly available. These have silver scales on a black, red, and white body.

An exceptionally fine champion Ginrin Kohaku with a great red pattern and wonderful metallic scales.

A wonderful group of six Kinginrin champions showing some of the variations acceptable in this grouping.

Koromo
    This variety has a blue or silver overlay on a red and white background.

Wow! What a magnificent fish. Its basic Kohaku pattern is overlaid with blue giving this Koromo a startling color design.

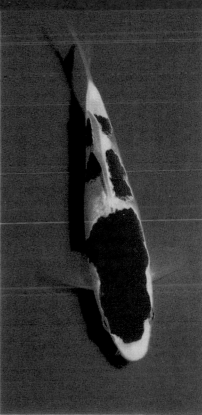

Six champion quality Koromo Koi showing various degrees of blue enhancing their basic Kohaku patterns.

Utsurimono

The body color of this variety is black with yellow, red, or white markings. The Hi Utsuri type is probably the most stunning form with bright red splashes of color on a black background, although the Ki Utsuri type with orange or yellow markings can be very dramatic as well. Doitsu types are also available.

The Utsurimono is a fish which is supposed to have more black than any other color. There may be some close calls between this variety and the Bekko. Modern judges say if the black is more prominent, even though less abundant, the fish can be called Utsurimono.

Six examples of modern Utsurimono champions. The fish above right is a world champion because of the judges' fantasies concerning its color pattern. When these fish are judged, the judges make remarks about what they *see* in the fish's pattern. This fish's pattern may have shown clouds forming before a storm.

Showa

This variety is also referred to as Showa Sanshoku and it is one of the most beautiful of all the Koi types. The body and head are mottled black, red, and white. The pectoral fins are black. Doitsu and leather types are known.

Six champion Showa Sanshoku. The term *showa* refers to a period during which a particular emperor ruled Japan. The *sanshoku* refers to the three-colored pattern. Judges fantasize about each color pattern. They see things in just the red, for example. Many consider this fish as a Kohaku with added black trimmings.

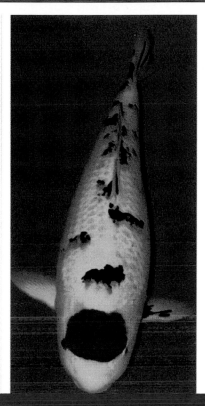

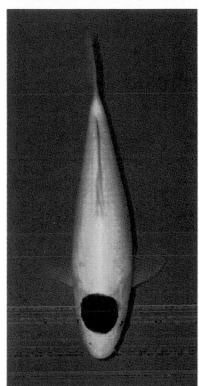

Tancho

The distinctive characteristic of this Koi is a brilliant red marking on the head. Otherwise the fish is usually of the purest white. The head blotch, however, can be combined with a variety of other Koi colors such as Tancho Showa, Tancho Utsuri and Tancho Sanke, all of which have the distinctive head blotch combined with the normal colors associated with these types of Koi.

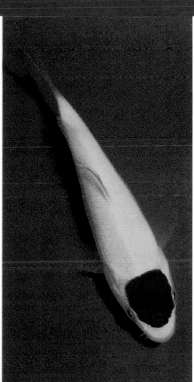

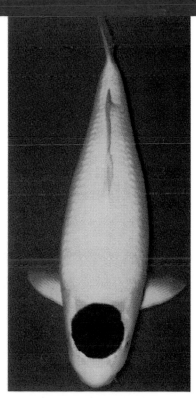

These show six champion Hikari. The term *Hikari* refers to the metallic scales. Other adjectives are used to describe whether they are one color (Hikari Mujimono, upper right and lower right), or some other recognizable color characteristic.

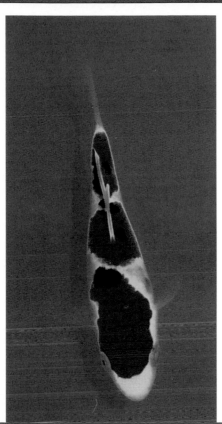

Taisho Sanshoku

This is very similar to the Showa but the black color is limited to the upper part of the fish with the pectoral fins being mostly white. Doitsu and Leather also exist in this variety.

Ogon

The Ogon is one of the better known varieties which can often be found for sale through normal trade outlets rather than specialist Koi shops. It has a lovely metallic gold coloration which can range from a light to a very dark gold color. However, a black cast to the color is a fault. Doitsu-like leather types are known and some of the Butterfly Koi approach this form in coloration as well.

Breeding Koi

Despite the high price and great mystique which surrounds them, Koi are actually very easy to breed. In the past all the top quality Koi were bred in Japan, but in recent times other Koi breeding centers have been developing. America now produces some good quality fish, as does the U.K., and this situation will improve even more as these breeders gain experience and knowledge. At the moment, the real problem arises when it comes to producing show quality fish of a particular type. These have to be of a specific color pattern to be any good at all, and the art of producing certain colored fish is known only to a few skilled breeders in Japan who are not going to give away their secrets.

Sexing juvenile Koi is just about impossible, so unless you buy an adult pair, which is very costly, you are going to have to wait until your fish are about 3 years old before you will know what sexes you have. For this reason, it is best to buy a group of 6 youngsters of the color type you want to breed and allow them to grow up together. Then you can select the best male and female from this group to use as breeders.

Mature Koi can be sexed by looking at their general body and fin shape. Males are more slender than females and their pectoral fins are more pointed. During early spring, they also develop small white pimples on the pectoral fins which are present right through the breeding season from late spring to early fall.

Once you have determined you have both sexes, you now need to set up a breeding pond. This should be at least 6 ft. square and about 2' 6" deep. If you have room, a larger pond would be better. A fully mature well conditioned female Koi can produce over 400,000 eggs, and although not all of these will hatch, you can comfortably expect thousands of babies to be produced from one spawning. The larger your breeding pond the more young you will be able to raise and the better chance you will have of rearing some good quality fish.

You need some way of covering your breeding pond with heavy plastic netting which is held firmly in place. A rigid wooden frame which is large enough to be fitted over the whole of the pond is one effective method. The reason for this netting is because Koi often jump clean out of the water when mating, and it would be a tragedy to find your best pair of Koi lying dried out by the side of the pond. It will also protect the fry from predators.

Your breeding pond should be cleaned out over the winter and filled with clean water during early spring. A couple of weeks after filling it with water some small crustaceans of the genus *Daphnia* can be introduced. These will feed on the green algae which inevitably develop in any body of water which is not filtered and has no growing plants in it. Be careful to only introduce daphnia in the pond; it is all too easy to miss a few dragonfly larvae or other predators which will eat your baby Koi later on.

With the coming of spring, temperatures will rise and Koi start to eat more. Once the water temperature has reached 60° F you can start conditioning your breeders. At this time, make sure you feed lots of good quality food. Koi pellets can form the basis of their diet but try to feed protein rich foods like shrimps and clams as well. This will help the female produce large quantities of eggs.

By late spring to early summer your female should be filled with eggs and ready to move into the breeding pond. You should also add something for the pair to spawn on. In America branches of Redwood trees are tied together to form giant spawning mops, but some conifer trees are poisonous to fish and must not be used. Personally I prefer artificial spawning mops made of 3' long pieces of nylon wool tied together into large bunches. These must be carefully washed before use and dropped into the pond a few days before the male fish is added. This will give them time to become waterlogged and sink to the bottom.

When everything is ready and your female has settled

into her new quarters, the male can be added late one evening. Most pairs will spawn early the next morning or within a few days. Courtship is very vigorous with the pair dashing about the pond and every so often coming together to deposit a batch of eggs. Most of these end up in or near the mops, but the adults are not too picky about this. Once spawning has finished the adults should be removed.

In about a week the eggs will hatch, but the fry do not become free swimming until a couple more days have gone by. Initially they need small live foods like small daphnia and newly hatched brine shrimp. The more they are fed at this stage the stronger and more robust the babies will be, so try to feed the pond at least three times a day. However, do not put too many brine shrimp in at one time because any left uneaten will die and pollute the water. After a few weeks, the babies can be fed on commercial fry and growth foods supplemented with live daphnia.

Now the pond will need some filtration and aeration added. This should not be too vigorous, and the filter's intake will need fine netting over the end to prevent babies from being sucked into it. Ten percent water changes should also be instigated at this time.

At a month old, any deformed or weak fry can be culled. At 3 months old you can start culling for color. Initially select for overall color and ignore any patterning. When assessing your fry, make sure you have photo-

graphs of top quality fish of the strain in front of you. Never rely on your memory of what you think the fish should look like.

Scalation can also be assessed at the three month

This magnificent champion is categorized in Japan as an Hikari-moyomono. With Koi it seems that *beauty lies in the eyes of the beholder*, that's what makes them so interesting.

stage, so remove any Doitsu fish with poor scale patterns. During the coming months over-crowding will be the major enemy, so be hard with

your culling and only keep fish which are showing good potential. At about the 4 month stage, the color patterns of your Koi fry can be given their first assessment and any poor fish culled. By now, at least 50% of the fry will have been culled. If you have more than this left you have probably been too generous when assessing your fry. Every month, you will need to go back to the pond and remove a few more fish. By the end of the summer you should be down to only 10% of the original spawn.

This heavy culling is very hard to do, but it is essential if the fry you raise are going to be of good quality. Remember, for every one top quality Koi several thousand will fail to meet the standard. Initially the deformed and weak fry will have to be put down and the older fry sold as feeder fish. Later the culls will be large enough to be sold as young Koi and many of these fish will be recognizably of a particular Koi type. These can be sold to petshops and garden centres so you will have some return on them, but you must only keep the very best of any year's spawning for yourself.

One thing which you must never do is release surplus fish into local ponds and streams. Even those in public parks connect up with natural waterways and Koi can do untold damage to natural ecosystems. You may think you are doing the fish a favor by letting them live, but these feral populations of Koi and other ornamental fish may bring the hobby into disrepute.

Goldfish

Over the centuries the appearance of *Carassius auratus* has been changed beyond all recognition. This has been done by carefully selecting breeding stock from each generation, picking out any new sports or mutations as they appeared, and breeding from these oddballs. This has produced a huge range of varieties some of which can be kept in ponds all year round, whilst others must have winter protection. The following is a list of the varieties which are generally available in the hobby.

Bubble-eye Goldfish.

Bubble-eye

When it comes to strange and bizarre looking fish the Bubble-eye Goldfish deserves an award! For a start, it has two caudal and anal fins but no dorsal fin. It is, however, the large fluid filled sacs under the eyes which really make this fish stand out. These wobble and flop about in a really beautiful/ugly way depending upon your point of view. Ideally they should have a short deep body but most fish coming in through the trade are elongated.

Not suitable for the pond because of its delicate eyesacs.

Celestial Goldfish.

Celestial

The Celestial Goldfish gets its name from the way its enlarged eyes point upwards so it is always looking towards the sky. It is a short–bodied twin-tail variety that has no dorsal fin. It is not all that common in the trade, but does appear from time to time. Due to the peculiar eye development, this Goldfish is unable to compete with other fish for food and should only be kept on its own.

Needs winter protection.

Comet

This form is very similar to the Common Goldfish but the finnage is much larger and more elongated. In body form it tends to be slender and gives the impression of being a faster moving fish. In show quality specimens the tail will be equal to or greater than the

Fantail Goldfish.

body length but most fish available commercially fail to meet this standard. The most common color form seen in the trade is red and white. These fish are called Sarassa Comets but all Goldfish color forms are possible.

At home in the pond all year round.

Common Goldfish

This is probably the ancestor of all the other fancy Goldfish types. Essentially, it is just a gold version of the wild fish with fins and body form unaltered. The coloration is caused by the loss of black pigmentation (melanin) in skin above the

Common Goldfish.

scales. The gene which causes this pigment loss does not start to have an effect until the babies are several months old and it may even be years before some fish fully color. Up until this time the young Goldfish is a dull brown color.

At home in the pond all year round.

Fantail

This is an English version of the Ryukin, which is Japan's second most popular variety. The major difference between the two is the

Calico Fantail Goldfish.

body shape which in the fantail is shorter and more rounded than normal Goldfish (almost like an egg) but relatively smooth backed, whilst in the Ryukin the back is distinctly humped and the body much deeper. Both varieties have twin caudal and anal fins but the Ryukin tends to have larger, more rounded fins than the Fantail.

At home in the pond all year round although winter protection may be needed in particularly harsh climates.

Jikin or Peacock Goldfish

Jikin
Jikin Goldfish are twin-tailed fish in which the development of each tail is almost at a 90 degree angle to the body. As such, it resembles a spread peacock's tail and it is sometimes known as the Peacock Tail Goldfish. In body form, it is slightly deeper than a Common Goldfish. It comes in several different color forms but the most sought–after have a silvery white body with red lips and fins.

Lionhead Goldfish.

At home in the pond all year round, although it may be more susceptible to predation because it cannot swim as fast as other varieties.

Lionhead
When it comes to aristocracy the Lionhead is it as far as the Japanese are concerned. This fish is one of the more bizarre twin-tail types in that the dorsal fin has been bred out of it. The head has also been selected for its broadness, and on the top and cheeks a large raspberry–like growth develops. The extent of this development will vary from fish to fish, but the bigger and better developed, the better as far as the breeders are concerned. All color varieties are known, although multicolored nacreous fish are rarely seen in the hobby.

Some winter protection is needed for this variety.

Black Moor Goldfish.

Black Moor
The Black Moor is another of my favorite Goldfish varieties. It is a velvety black fish with double tail and anal fins. You

usually see it in the telescope or globe eye form and in the U.K. it is particularly sought after, especially those with veiltail finnage. This type is known as the Broadtail Moor.

Needs some winter protection.

Oranda Goldfish.

Oranda
In most respects, this twin-tail Goldfish is similar to the Veiltail with similar finnage and body shape. The difference between the two varieties is a fleshy raspberry–like growth on the top of the head and around the cheeks. Good specimens will have this developed equally over all areas, but most imported fish have the hood development limited to the top of the head. One of the most common forms of this fish is the Red-cap Oranda, which has a red hood limited only to the top of the head and a silvery white body.

Needs some winter protection.

Pearlscale
This was one of the first fancy Goldfish I ever kept and I still have a soft spot for it today. In body shape it is very

Pearlscale Goldfish.

short and rotund and the twin tails are usually short and standing out well clear of the body. This unusual shape gave rise to the nick-name "Clock-work Orange" amongst aquarists in the south of England, because the tails looked just like a key sticking out of an orange. Apart from its shape, the distinctive characteristic of this variety is the domed scales. These look just like a string of pearls along the fish's flanks. A longer–finned form of this variety is known, and it is this form which you most often see offered for sale.

Needs some winter protection.

Fantail Goldfish with Pompons.

Pompon

I am not a great lover of those varieties which do not have a dorsal fin, but this fish is one I would like to work with in the future. It has a short deep body form with twin-tail and anal fins. Its characteristic feature is the development of pompons above each nostril. These are known as narial bouquets, and in some individuals are developed to a tremendous degree.

Needs some winter protection.

Ryukin

This is Japan's second most popular Goldfish variety and is favored by Goldfish breeders because of all the twin-tailed types it tends to produce more good quality fish per brood than any other. The back is distinctly humped and the fins

Ryukin Goldfish.

are larger than normal Goldfish. The tail should be completely divided into two fins as should the anal fin.

At home in the pond all year round.

Shubunkin Goldfish.

Shubunkins

Shubunkins are actually multicolored or nacreous Goldfish. They have a mix of blue, black, brown, red, white, and yellow colors on their body. In body form they are similar to the Common Goldfish or Comet and can have the normal finnage of a Common Goldfish (London Shubunkins) or have enlarged fins like Comets (Japanese or Comet Shubunkins). There is also a variety called Bristol Shubunkin which has enlarged finnage, but unlike the Comet types where the fins are long and pointed, they have rounded tips and the body tends to be more stocky. London and Bristol Shubunkins are named for the areas in the U.K. where these types were developed.

At home in the pond all year round.

Veiltail

This is an egg–shaped twin-tail variety which is considered

Veiltail Goldfish.

by some (myself included) as the most beautiful of all Goldfish. The tail is usually long and broad with straight leading edges. Good specimens have completely divided tails and anal fins (although this can be difficult to see because the tails hang down and obscure your view of the anal fins). Veiltails come in all color forms, but can be hard to find because they are not generally commercially bred.

Aquarium maintenance only.

Wakin Goldfish.

Wakin

The Wakin is the common Goldfish of Japan. In body form, it tends to be a little deeper than the Common Goldfish but the finnage is similar in size. The caudal fin is doubled to some degree and in good specimens will actually form two tails with the anal fin also doubled. It comes in all color forms and is gaining popularity in the UK where it commands a high price despite often being found as a contaminant amongst a shipment of normal Shubunkins.

At home in the pond all year round.

Other Fish

There is a huge range of other fish which can be kept in a pond. The variety available to you may be quite limited because many species are just not seen for sale in aquatic outlets. This is a real shame because we are missing out on some lovely creatures.

Care should be taken to quarantine all fish properly, but if you suspect they have come from the wild you must take particular precautions against diseases entering your pond. Extend the quarantine period to a month and keep a close watch on the animals concerned.

It is worth remembering that many countries have strict rules on what can be taken out of the wild for ornamental purposes. If you plan to catch fish in the wild for introduction to your pond, check with your local Fish and Wildlife Department to make sure you are not breaking the law.

The following is a list of those species which you see from time to time offered for sale in aquatic outlets:

American Fathead Minnows (*Pimephales promelas*)
These interesting fish only grow to about 5" and are

Pimephales promelas.

usually seen in the attractive golden form. They tend to spend much of their time near the surface of the pond and feed on all types of foods including flake and pond pellets. A worthy addition for small and medium sized ponds.

Rhodeus amarus.

Bitterling (*Rhodeus amarus*)
Bitterling are more often kept in a coldwater aquarium than in an outdoor pond, but they will live quite happily in this environment as well. Reaching only some 3" when full grown, it is one of the smaller inhabitants and can only be kept with non-predatory fish which will not pose a threat to it. They eat all foods and make ideal inhabitants of a small pond with goldfish.

Bream (*Abramis brama*)
Bream are rarely included in an ornamental pond because of their size which can

Abramis brama.

exceed 30". If you have a large enough pond, they can be useful as scavengers because they rummage through the substrate searching out food other fish have missed. Unfortunately they tend to soil the water as they do this which can have a detrimental effect on water clarity.

Cyprinus carpio.

Carp (*Cyprinus carpio*)
These are the wild form of Koi and need the same sort of conditions. Being plain brown colored, from above you will only see them when they come up to feed, but they can be trained to feed directly from your hand.

Ictalurus punctatus.

Channel Cats (*Ictalurus punctatus*)
Channel Cats are sometimes called Blue Cats and they come in both normal and albino colors. It is a predatory creature which will eat any fish small enough to fit in its mouth, and at 3' long when full grown there are few fish too large for its mouth.

Alburnoides bipunctatus.

Chub (*Alburnoides bipunctatus*)

Chub are one of the smaller schooling fish which make a suitable addition to the garden pond when kept in a group of 10 to 20. They need well oxygenated water so good filtration is a must; they eat all foods including flake so are easy to accommodate otherwise. Although they are only a light brownish color when viewed from above, they do spend most of their time near the surface so can be seen in a pond.

Carassius auratus.

Crucian Carp (*Carassius carassius*)

Crucian Carp are very close relatives of common Goldfish and need the same sort of conditions. They tend to grow larger than Goldfish and can reach 20" in a large pond. Since they are a plain silvery brown from above, you are unlikely to see them very often.

Golden Orfe (*Leuciscus idus*)

Golden Orfe are very popular pond fish which are commonly sold for garden ponds. They are shoaling predators which feed on small fish and

Leuciscus idus.

insect life, but are peaceful with anything which they cannot fit in their mouths. In captivity they grow to about 18" long, but the wild form can reach up to 3' in length. They like well oxygenated water and can be sensitive to water treatments.

Gobio gobio.

Gudgeon (*Gobio gobio*)

Gudgeon are supposed to be bottom dwelling scavengers which sieve through the substrate looking for food. Unfortunately no one seems to have told the fish that. In fact, they spend a great deal of time in the mid-water region of a pond and only dive to the bottom when they have been frightened or are following food down. At about 8" when full grown they make good additions to smaller ponds but they are sensitive to water pollution so can only be kept in filtered ponds.

Minnows (*Phoxinus phoxinus*)

Minnows come from flowing clear water with a high oxygen content and need similar

Phoxinus phoxinus.

conditions to thrive in captivity. They can be included in a pond only if good filtration is used, and since they are a shoaling fish it is best to keep them in groups of 20 to 100. In the wild, they feed on small insect life and other living foods so may take some time to adjust to commercially produced alternatives.

Rutilus rutilus.

Roach (*Rutilus rutilus*)

This is a shoaling fish which is basically silver on the body with pale orange fins. It grows to about 16" and likes clean well filtered water. It is an omnivore which will eat any food offered.

Rudd (*Scardineus erythrophthalmus*)

Rudd grow up to about 16" and are a peaceful shoaling species. The body color is

Scardineus erythrophthalmus.

basically silvery but a golden form does exist. Both forms have orangery fins with the pelvic, anal, and caudal fins bright red.

Tinca tinca.

Silurus glanis.

Tench (*Tinca tinca*)

Tench tend to be overlooked by many aquatic outlets yet they make excellent additions to the garden pond. Being bottom dwellers, they spend much of their time grubbing about the substrate searching for any morsels of food which the other fish missed. Even though they perform this vital role as a scavenger you must also make sure your tench are fed properly. Many pond pellets are designed to float until eaten, which is fine for surface feeders but will cause your tench to starve to death. The golden form is by far the best for pond situations since the natural green form is invisible in a pond.

Three-spined Sticklebacks (*Gasterosteus aculeatus*)

Three-spined sticklebacks are one of the most ignored of all coldwater fish and yet a male in full breeding regalia is a truly breathtaking sight. They make ideal additions to small wildlife ponds but should be carefully quarantined for a month before introduction. This is because they can be riddled with parasites if they have been caught in the wild.

Wels Catfish (*Siluris glanis*)

Sometimes I wonder at the lack of common sense shown by a small element in the aquatic trade. Of all the most unsuitable fish which could be offered for sale for a garden pond this has to be the worst and yet it is the one I have seen most often. Wels Catfish are predatory monsters which grow up to 9 ft. in body length and will make a meal of even full grown Koi.

Three-spined Stickleback, *Gasterosteus aculeatus.*